I CAN PLAY SPORTS!

Skateboarding

by Thomas Kingsley Troupe

Kaleidoscope
Minneapolis, MN

Where the Quest for Discovery Begins

This edition first published in 2023 by Kaleidoscope Publishing, Inc.

Kaleidoscope Publishing, Inc.
6012 Blue Circle Drive
Minnetonka, MN 55343

Library of Congress Control Number
2022938028

ISBN
978-1-64519-585-6 (library bound)
978-1-64519-655-6 (ebook)

Bigfoot Jr. lurks within one of the images in this book. It's up to you to find him!

Table of Contents

Half Pipe

The **skater** hops onto the skateboard. It's time to do tricks! The skater rolls down the **ramp**.

The board picks up speed. The skater jumps and flips the board. I can skateboard!

Skateboarding is usually done at a **skate park**. Skate parks are built indoors or outside.

Most skate parks have ramps and rails. They are built so skaters can do tricks and **stunts**.

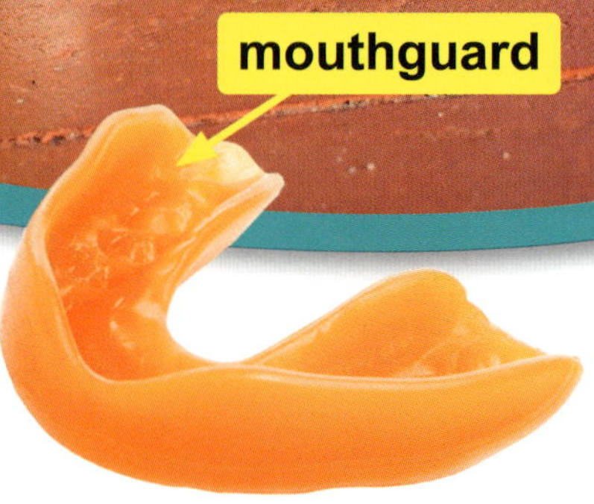

Skaters should wear helmets on their heads. A **mouthguard** protects their teeth from **injury**.

Skateboarders wear knee pads and elbow pads too. They keep skaters from getting hurt.

FUN FACT

Skateboarding was invented in California in the 1950s.

Meet the Skater

Skateboarding is a **solo** sport. Skaters try moves and tricks on their skateboard.

To be a good skateboarder, it takes practice. Staying on the board can be very hard!

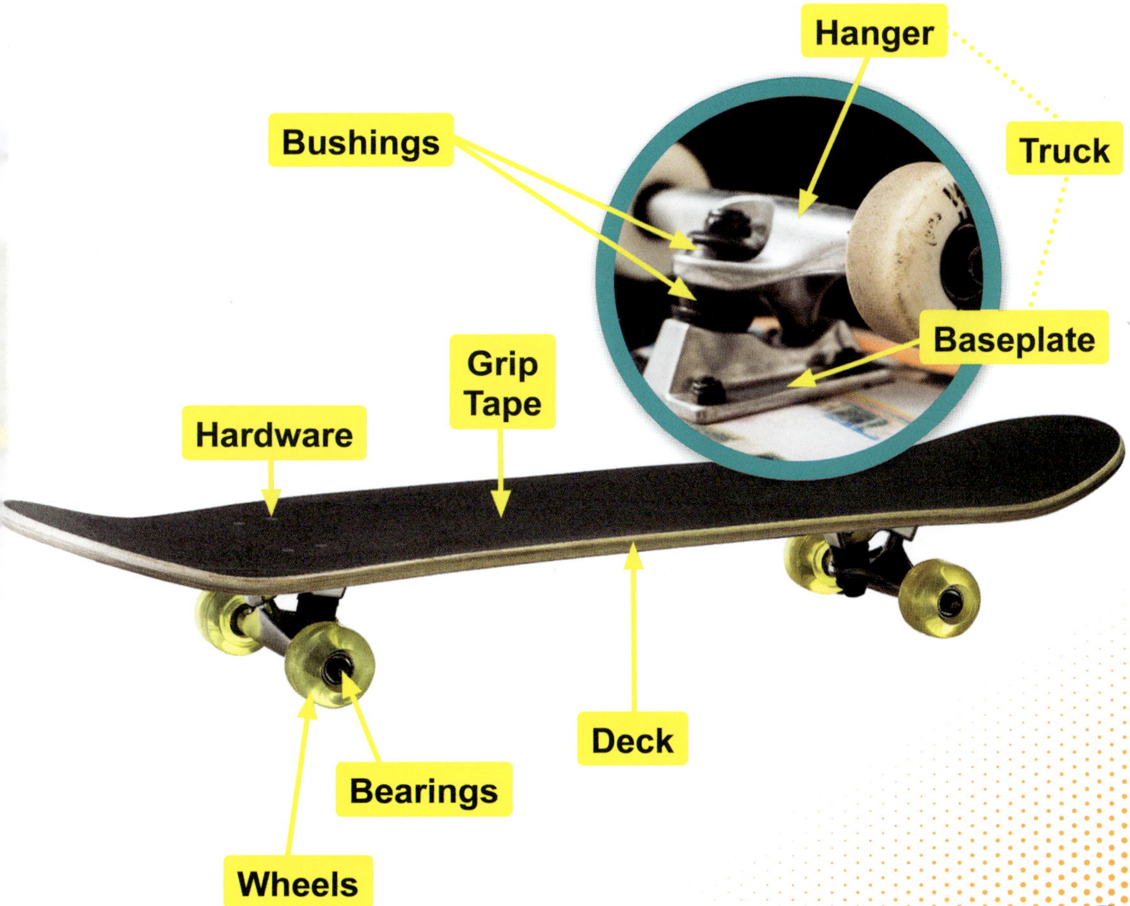

Some skaters skateboard with friends. They can teach each other new stunts to try out.

Skaters might make videos of their tricks. They watch the videos to learn from their mistakes.

FUN FACT

There are around 3,100 skate parks in the United States.

Amazing Run

A manual is a type of trick. It's when a skateboarder rides with only two wheels on the ground.

An ollie is a skateboard jump. The skater and board lift up into the air together.

FUN FACT

Skateboarding used to be called "sidewalk surfing."

There are five basic skills in skateboarding

1 Pushing

using a leg to move the skateboard forward

2 Stopping

coming to a stop on a skateboard

3 Turning

leaning to turn the board to the left or right

4 Balance

staying on the board without falling off

5 Manual

riding on the front or back two wheels

A grind is sliding a skateboard along an edge. Skaters often grind on cement walls and curbs.

Some skaters can flip their skateboard. They jump and the board flips under their feet.

Kick Flip!

Some skateboarders will **compete** against other skaters. They perform tricks for **judges** and a crowd.

The judges score and give points for great stunts. Skaters lose points for falling or doing bad tricks.

Skateboarding was added to the Olympic Games in 2020.

Skaters often get three tries to do their best tricks. The judges use the best score for each skater.

The skater with the highest score wins. But, all the skaters had fun. Let’s try skateboarding again!

Photo Glossary

compete: When people take part in a contest.

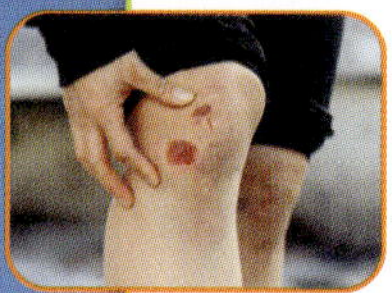

injury: Damage to someone's body that can cause pain or broken bones. Skaters wear gear to protect them from injury.

judges: The people who score sporting events.

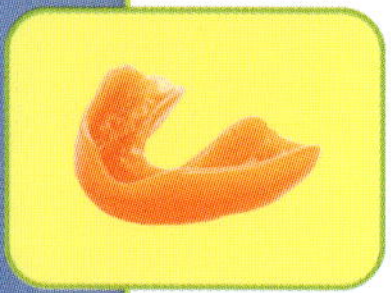

mouthguard: The piece of plastic that skaters wear to protect their teeth.

ramp: A slope or hill that is used to build speed in a skate park.

skate park: A paved area that is designed for skateboarders to practice.

skater: A person who uses a skateboard.

solo: When someone does something alone, by themselves.

stunts: The tricks that skaters use to get attention.

Read More

Abdo, Kenny. *Skateboarding.* Mankato, MN, ABDO Publishing, 2018.

Latchana Kenney, Karen. *Extreme Skateboarding Challenges.* Minneapolis, MN, Lerner Publishing, 2021.

McClellan, Ray. *Skateboarding.* Hopkins, MN, Bellwether Media, 2011.

Websites

FACTSURFER

Factsurfer.com gives you a safe, fun way to find more information.

1. Go to www.factsurfer.com.
2. Enter "Skateboarding" into the search box and click 🔍
3. Select your book cover to see a list of related websites.

About the Author

Thomas Kingsley Troupe has been reading and writing stories from a very young age. He's the author of over 100 books for kids of all ages. When he's not putting words together, he's fixing his house, watching movies, ghost-hunting or thinking about taking a nap. Thomas lives in Woodbury, MN, with his two ridiculous sons.

INDEX

PHOTO CREDITS

The images in this book are reproduced through the courtesy of: Izf/Shutterstock Images, cover (top); al7/Shutterstock Images, cover, 1; ShotPrime Studio/Shutterstock Images, cover, 1 (girl); xiaorui/Shutterstock Images, p. 3; Christian Vinces/Shutterstock Images, p. 4–5; Rose Hayes/Shutterstock Images, p. 5; REDPIXEL.PL/Shutterstock Images, p. 6–7, 22 (skate park); kornnphoto/Shutterstock Images, p. 8; Andrii Zhmendak/Shutterstock Images, p. 8, 22 (mouthguard); supawat bursuk/Shutterstock Images, p. 9; karen roach/Shutterstock Images, p. 9 (Fun Fact); COLOMBO NICOLA/Shutterstock Images, p. 10; fotoslaz/Shutterstock Images, p. 11; Golubovy/Shutterstock Images, p. 11 (circle); fotoliza/Shutterstock Images, p. 12; Rick Becker-Leckrone/Shutterstock Images, p. 13; 19 STUDIO/Shutterstock Images, p. 13 (phone); Izf/Shutterstock Images, p. 14–15, 22 (solo); yanik88/Shutterstock Images, p. 15; NassornSnitwong/Shutterstock Images, p. 15 (Fun Fact); progressman/Shutterstock Images, p. 16 (pushing); metaldom77/Shutterstock Images, p. 16 (stopping); kornnphoto/Shutterstock Images, p. 16 (turning); Elizaveta Galitckaia/Shutterstock Images, p. 16 (balance); yanik88/Shutterstock Images, p. 16 (manual); homydesign/Shutterstock Images, p. 17, 22 (stunts); FiledIMAGE/Shutterstock Images, p. 18; Will Rodrigues/Shutterstock Images, p. 19 (top); A.RICARDO/Shutterstock Images, p. 19, 22 (compete); YamabikaY/Shutterstock Images, A.RICARDO/Shutterstock Images, p.20, p. 22 (ramp); mikeforemniakowski/Shutterstock Images, p. 22 (skater); New Africa/Shutterstock Images, p. 22 (judges); Izf/Shutterstock Images, p. 22 (injury); Nor Gal/Shutterstock Images, p. 23.